Ghost Walks around York

over 50 of York's haunted locations

David Shaw

Published by Sigma Leisure – an imprint of Sigma Press, Stobart House, Pontyclerc, Penybanc Road Ammanford, Carmarthenshire SA18 3HP

British Library Cataloguing in Publication Data

A CIP record for this book is available from the British Library

ISBN: 978-1-85058-868-9

Typesetting and Design by: Sigma Press, Ammanford, Wales

Maps: © Bute Cartographics

Photographs: © David Shaw

Cover photograph: York Minster © David Shaw

Printed by: TJ International Ltd

Disclaimer: The information in this book is given in good faith and is believed to be correct at the time of publication. Care should always be taken when walking in hill country. Where appropriate, attention has been drawn to matters of safety. The author and publisher cannot take responsibility for any accidents or injury incurred whilst following these walks. Do not rely solely on sketch maps for navigation: we strongly recommend the use of appropriate Ordnance Survey (or equivalent) maps.

Ghost Walks
around York

Cui dono lepidum novum libellum?

To my wife Janet, for making our many stays in York
such happy times.

Contents

Walk 3: Around the hanted walls 57

But is York really haunted? 95

Introduction

For over twenty years I have been a regular visitor to the beautiful and historic city of York and during my many pleasant stays I gradually became aware of the enormous wealth of reported ghost sightings in the area. Personally, I can testify to one such experience and can think of no better place in which to undertake a walk through haunted sites, yet remain in the midst of such stunning surroundings. Having so many ghost sightings within its ancient walls, York richly deserves its reputation as the most haunted city in the world. I have long loved both walking around this uniquely magical location and hearing chilling tales of its ghostly past. As I wandered across Lendal bridge one morning the notion hit me: what better than to bring the two elements together in a book?

In my experience, small groups are certainly more appropriate than large parties on ghost walks, especially if you are hoping to see or hear something paranormal. The sites may, of course, be walked in daylight but if you prefer a more atmospheric amble, I would suggest a starting time of one hour before nightfall, so that you are enveloped by the dark as you progress, but please take the usual safety precautions that you would on any evening out and bring along a small torch in order to read the text.

A word of caution: Please respect the privacy of the occupants of the various private buildings on our walk. Don't disturb them by knocking on their doors and, of course, don't trespass on any property. This is not only common courtesy, there is also an ulterior motive for this good behaviour: remember that one day in the future these people may also pass into the spirit world and I'm sure none of us would want to incur their wrath.

David Shaw
September 2012

Walk One:

The City Centre

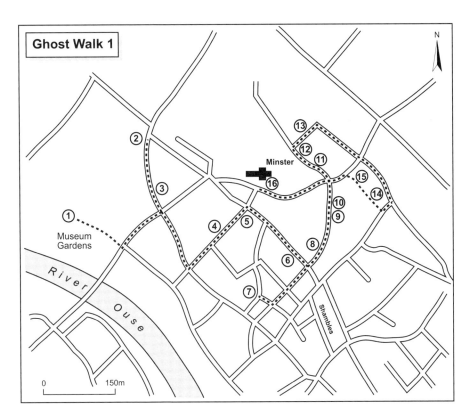

1. Yorkshire Museum
2. King's Manor
3. Theatre Royal
4. Ye Olde Starre Inne
5. 41 Stonegate
6. Lund's Court
7. Roman Bath
8. Holy Trinity

9. Snickleway Inn
10. Tudor House
11. St. William's College
12. 5 College Street
13. Treasurer's House
14. Bedern
15. Bedern Archway
16. York Minster

Let's begin our tour by entering the perennially pleasant Museum Gardens through the gates in Museum Street. Continue straight on; the Yorkshire Museum is on the right.

The Yorkshire Museum

1. Yorkshire Museum
(Gardens open until 8pm in summer, until dusk in winter)

We find ourselves standing in front of the impressive stone pillars of the Yorkshire Museum. It was in the former library of this building that our first ghost sighting occurred. In September 1953, the museum's caretaker was shocked to see an old man in a frock coat wandering amongst the shelves after closing time, repeating to himself "I must find it". As the caretaker approached the man, he vanished. Four weeks later the same figure was seen again, crossing the hall and walking through locked doors into the library (now the museum gift shop).

To investigate the apparition, a panel of observers were brought in for a session, including a doctor and a solicitor. They did not see the ghost, but during their evening vigil the temperature noticeably dropped and a book rose from the shelf of its own accord. The volume was called *Antiquities and Curiosities of the Church* and it had been presented to the library by a solicitor from Darlington, Alderman Edward Wooler, who had died in 1921. Was this the figure seen by the caretaker and had he finally found what he was seeking?

Retrace your steps back through the gates and turn left back into Museum Street. Take the first turning on the left into St. Leonard's Place and continue straight on until you reach the beautiful square with fountains in front of the Art Gallery. King's Manor is through the gateway on your left.

2. The King's Manor

This historic series of buildings has, as you would expect, generated several reports of ghostly apparitions. A phantom monk is said to wander through the interior, a reminder that part of it used to belong to the nearby St. Mary's Abbey, which now lies in ruins in the Museum Gardens.

Also seen was a lady in a green Tudor-style dress. She materialised out of a cupboard, carrying a bunch of flowers. It was later realised that the wing in which the ghost appeared is built over a former rose garden.

Another phantom which is seen from time to time in the King's Manor is believed to be the ghost of Thomas Wentworth, a seventeenth century gentleman who was arrested here and eventually beheaded on a charge of treason against King Charles I. The figure of a grey man in Stuart costume wanders the stairs and rooms of this historic mansion. This apparition was also seen by four teachers who held a

The King's Manor

midnight vigil inside the former school one Halloween before World War II, but when the headmaster, annoyed at their ghost-watch, burst into the room the figure vanished.

Turn back along St. Leonard's Place and cross the road. In front of you is the impressive façade of the Theatre Royal.

3. The Theatre Royal

A shadowy grey lady has been seen on many occasions over the years inside the theatre, sometimes in dressing rooms, sometimes in the auditorium. It is believed that her origins lie in the former St. Leonard's Hospital, since the Theatre Royal is built over its ruins. The grey lady is thought to be the ghost of a nun who claimed to have seen angels at mass. For 'lying' she was given the rather excessive

The Theatre Royal

punishment of being bricked into one of the walls while she was still alive. Imagine her nightmare of torment as she slowly deteriorated, dying from thirst and hunger, trapped in the claustrophobic space behind the stones.

The nun's horrific demise seems not to have turned her into a malevolent spirit since nowadays actors take her appearance as a favourable omen which augurs well for a successful production. She has been seen in her grey habit leaning over the edge of a box by the stage.

Continue along St. Leonard's Place, cross over the road into Blake Street and, as you reach St. Helen's Square, turn left up into Stonegate. As you walk up this ancient street you cannot fail to notice the wooden sign overhead marking the entrance to Ye Olde Starre Inne, which lies through a passageway on your left.

4. Ye Olde Starre Inne

Two ghostly black cats have been seen inside this fine old inn from time to time and dogs have been known to growl at an unseen presence in the bar. There are reports of an old lady occasionally glimpsed on the stairs by young children, though her identity is unknown.

More disturbing are the unearthly cries of pain which are sometimes heard echoing through this building. After the battle of Marston Moor was fought to the west of York during the civil war in 1644, wounded Roundheads were brought to the cellar of the Starre Inne where they were treated according to the brutal and primitive medical practices of the time. The disembodied screams of those military casualties from centuries ago are said to still fill the air, a ghostly reminder of the agonies they suffered.

Ye Olde Starre Inne

In fact there are many reported sightings of ghostly roundheads and cavaliers in the fields around the village of Long Marston near the site of the battle. In 1932 on a foggy November night two men were driving along a lane in the area when they became aware of several men in hats, cloaks and boots walking at the roadside. They stopped the car and got out to investigate, but the figures had simply vanished.

Continue along Stonegate, our next destination is number 41, a shop on the right.

5. 41 Stonegate

Although currently an antiques centre, in Victorian times this house was the home of a doctor, his wife and their young daughter. One evening the doctor was hosting a dinner party which his daughter was reluctant to leave at her bedtime. Nevertheless, she was sent up to her

41 Stonegate

bedroom on the top floor of the house but as she reached the highest landing she could not resist leaning over the banister to hear the sound of the merriment below. Unfortunately, the little girl leaned too far, lost her balance and plummeted down through the open stairwell, falling to her death on the basement floor.

The ghost of a little girl in Victorian dress has been seen sitting on the counter and wandering around the shop. Often small objects are moved to a new position by invisible fingers, the little girl apparently at play once more.

At the top of Stonegate turn right into Low Petergate. As you continue, look for a small passageway on your right marked 'Lund's Court'. Walk down the alleyway into the small courtyard.

6. Lund's Court

Lund's Court

This charming courtyard hides a tragic past, for it was here that Alice Smith lived in the early 19th century with her cruel and insensitive husband. Tired of being the butt of his constant brutality, one day something inside her snapped and she murdered her tormentor. When her crime was discovered she was declared insane and hanged at York Castle in 1825.

After such a traumatic existence in this world it is perhaps unsurprising that her ghost has been seen in the place where she used to live. She is seen at the window, looking down into the courtyard where you are standing, her face distraught with terror.

Retrace your steps back down the passageway, turn right and continue along Low Petergate. At the end of the road turn right into Church Street; take the second turning on your right into St. Sampson's Square and a little further ahead on your right is the Roman Bath.

The Roman Bath

7. The Roman Bath

This fascinating pub is surely unique since it was constructed on top of the remains of a Roman military bath house. Amazingly, it is still possible to visit the ancient baths, housed in the museum under the pub. However, visitors to the archaic ruins have reported a great deal of unusual activity among its age-old stones.

Inexplicably, strange white spheres of light have emerged out of the walls and shadowy figures are seen to flit about the different rooms of the bath house. A soldier from the civil war has also been seen wandering through the historic chambers where Roman soldiers once bathed and relaxed.

Retrace your path back into Church Street and continue straight on into Goodramgate. A short distance ahead of you on the left are the gates of Holy Trinity Church inside a brick archway.

8. Holy Trinity

A lady came to eat her sandwiches in the churchyard of Holy Trinity one lunch time, sitting down on a bench. After a while she looked up to see the back of a man in Elizabethan dress who seemed to have his head bowed, looking at the gravestones. As he slowly made his way around the yard she reasoned that he must be on a break from some theatrical production. It was only when he turned around to face her that she realised the truth: the man was not stooping, he had no head.

This ghost has been sighted on other occasions and is believed to be Thomas Percy, an Elizabethan gentleman who led a failed Catholic rebellion. As a result he was executed in 1572 and his head was cut off and displayed on a spike on top of Micklegate Bar. His body was buried in the churchyard of St. Crux at the bottom of the Shambles, but two years later his head was stolen from the spike by a sympathetic servant and buried somewhere in the grounds of Holy Trinity. Is this why his phantom is seen wandering around the graveyard, as if trying to locate his severed head?

Holy Trinity

Continue along Goodramgate; ahead on the right you will find the Snickleway Inn.

9. Snickleway Inn

This historic pub, for many years better known under its former name 'The Anglers Arms', is reputed to be haunted by several ghosts. Spirits are often connected to strange smells, which come and go suddenly, and that is the case here where the scent of lavender inexplicably fills the upstairs rooms. A Victorian child is sometimes seen on the stairs, thought to be the victim of a tragic accident which occurred when she ran out of the pub into the path of a passing cart.

In the low-roofed cellar is a more malevolent presence connected with poltergeist activity such as turning off the taps on the beer barrels and moving objects.

The Snickleway Inn

Next to The Snickleway Inn is the timber-framed Tudor House.

10. Tudor House

Although this building is now an Italian restaurant, it has a long history and has been the scene of unexplained activity. Doors open by themselves and lights are turned on by unseen hands. An explanation was discovered, while renovation work was being carried out in an upstairs room, in the form of an inscription scratched into the old plaster:

Marmaduke Buckle

1715

1697

17

Marmaduke, a disabled young man, lived in the house in the Eighteenth century and it seems that tragically he recorded his date of birth and death in the plaster before hanging himself from a beam in the upstairs chamber at the age of seventeen.

Continue straight on and cross the junction with Deangate, turning left into College Street. St. William's College is on your right.

Tudor House

11. St. William's College

In the 17th century some parts of this beautiful timber-framed institution were rented out to poorer residents of York, who lived here among the more wealthy clergymen. Two brothers who had an upper room here were short of money and the older one hatched a wicked scheme to attack and rob one of the clerics. His younger sibling was uneasy about the plan, but eventually he was convinced and they ambushed the unsuspecting churchman in a narrow alleyway and took his purse. But in the struggle the older brother took out a knife and stabbed their victim to death, to the utter horror of the younger man.

They hastened back to their room in St William's College, where he expressed his grave misgivings, causing the older brother to fear that he was about to go to the authorities and make a confession. Instead,

St.William's College

he himself turned informer and painted his younger brother as the main perpetrator in return for his own pardon. The younger brother was hanged for the crime and his older sibling was left to pace the corridors of the College wracked by guilt over his terrible deeds, until he could stand it no longer and hanged himself. His ghostly footsteps are still heard at night, echoing through the old building as if his spirit is condemned to wander up and down the passageways, contemplating his misdeeds.

Continue along College Street and stop at the stone house on the corner.

12. 5 College Street

This historic stone building, in the shadow of the Minster, has a terrible past. In the 1950s a family with young children moved into the house, but the domestic bliss was soon shattered by paranormal

5 College Street

activity. An upstairs room with a small window was the children's bedroom and on several occasions at night the eerie sound of sobbing had filled the air, the cries apparently coming from nowhere. Then the children mentioned a little girl who sat on the end of the bed, in tears during the night. The children were moved into another room and the haunted bedroom was kept as the guest room!

The tragic history of 5 College Street was later uncovered. In the middle ages the house was occupied by a man, his wife and their young daughter. When the horrors of the plague were unleashed upon York, sadly the occupants of this dwelling were affected. The terrified locals, though, desperate to contain the spread of the disease, sealed up the doors and windows, locking the family inside with the plague. The mother and father perished from the effects of the pestilence but it transpired that their daughter was immune to the illness. This was not so fortunate since, imprisoned in the building with the rotting corpses of her parents, she was left to starve to death as the local people would not believe that she was free of the disease.

The distressed young girl is still seen at the window of this house today, and sometimes just her sobbing is audible drifting into the night, a terrible testament to the primitive brutality of a bygone age.

Continue straight on with the Minster on your left, then turn right into the cobbled Chapter House Street. Ahead on your left is the Treasurer's House.

13. Treasurer's House

This fine old building is the scene of York's most famous ghost story. In February 1953 a central heating system was being installed in the house and an eighteen-year-old apprentice, Harry Martindale, was sent into a small cellar to chisel a hole in the vaulted ceiling to house a pipe. He was up a ladder shortly before lunchtime, hammering at the cellar roof when he unexpectedly heard the sound of a horn blast, which gradually grew louder. He was perplexed to realise that it was coming out of the stone wall to the right of his ladder. As Harry looked down he suddenly saw a Roman soldier emerge from the wall, in military uniform and blowing on a short horn.

In shock, Harry fell back off his ladder and crawled into the corner of the small room watching in terror as about twenty Roman soldiers walked past him, including one on a sturdy cart horse. They seemed completely real, not spectral in any way, but they were not like the Hollywood Romans he had seen at the cinema. These men were tired, dishevelled and carried short swords and round shields, they had plumes above their metal helmets and wore skirts made of leather strips. They stood only about five feet tall although Harry could only see them from the knees up, until they passed through an archaeological trench which had been dug into the floor. In this lower area he saw their feet and lower legs, now walking on top of

The Treasurer's House

an actual excavated Roman road the *Via Decumana.* As the group passed by, Harry could discern their fatigued mutterings. They all disappeared into the opposite wall without being aware of Harry's presence. Terrified, the young man fled back along a passageway and up the cellar steps, where he sat in a state of shock. The elderly curator of the Treasurer's House saw him sitting there and, rather pleased, exclaimed "By the look of you you've seen the Roman soldiers!"

Unknown to Harry, there had been earlier sightings of the legionaries in the Treasurer's House. In the early 1900s a fancy dress party was being held there and during the evening one young lady wandered down to the cellar, only to find a Roman soldier in front of her barring her way into the passageway with his spear. Annoyed, she complained to her host about the rude guest dressed as a legionary, only to be told that no-one was wearing such a costume.

Nor was Harry's the last sighting. In February 1957 a lady was living in the Treasure's house with her husband and young daughter. Since it was particularly cold, she went down to the cellar to look at the central heating boiler but as she walked down the low passageway which leads to it, she became aware of someone behind her in the corridor. She turned around to see several Roman soldiers moving down the passage, some on horseback. Again, they were visible only from the knees up as they passed her, and again the Roman soldiers seemed tired, scruffy and demoralised. They disappeared as they rounded the corner of the passageway, the sound of hooves ringing in the dank air.

The famous cellar, where Harry Martindale saw those downhearted Roman soldiers 1500 years after their natural lives came to an end, is now open to the public as regular guided tours are available for visitors to the splendid Treasurer's House. When will these ghosts of ancient conquerors next be glimpsed here in York?

Continue down Chapter House Street and turn right into Ogleforth. Cross over the road and go straight on into Aldwark. At the Merchant Taylors' Hall turn right into St. Andrewgate. Shortly ahead of you on the right, between two modern houses, is a passageway marked 'Bedern'. Walk through it into the courtyard containing three trees.

14. Bedern

Although this part of York is now a modern housing development, it has a long history. The name 'Bedern' means 'house of prayer', reflecting the buildings of the Minster Vicars Choral Colleges which once filled the area, but by the 19th century it had become a slum plagued by over-crowding and poor sanitation. Where the trees now stand in the attractive new square, there used to be a workhouse – the York Industrial Ragged School – run by a man called Mr. Pimm. His institution housed the poor and orphaned children of the local area, for which Mr. Pimm was paid a sum of money for each youngster in his care. However, he neglected the children, leaving them undernourished and susceptible to the many diseases which were rife at the time. Gradually, the unfortunate young children began to die and Pimm, unwilling to accept a loss of income, buried their bodies in shallow graves in waste ground. But when in winter the ground

Bedern

became too hard to dig, he had to find another solution. Pimm hid the corpses of the poor infants in a cupboard at the bottom of the stairs, where they began to rot.

Then Pimm's cruelty and neglect caught up with him. Three or four of the dead children began to appear in front of him and were even seen playing in the street. Pimm was driven to drink and eventually became insane, finally taking his own life in a local asylum after his barbaric deeds had been discovered by the authorities.

But that was not the end of the story. In the 1980s Bedern was redeveloped with modern housing and many new paranormal events took place. The children have made their presence felt to many people in this area and this remains probably the most active haunted location in the city.

Continue on past the posts and go straight ahead with the old stone chapel on your left. Stop in front of the covered archway.

15. Bedern Archway

A man walking his dog past this archway just before midnight was surprised to hear the sound of children playing so late at night. He turned into the covered passageway but his dog would not follow him in. As he got to the other side of the arch the sound stopped abruptly – yet more evidence that the poor children of Bedern are still active.

Pass through the archway and turn left into Goodramgate, the right into Deangate. Follow the road ahead round the corner and stop by the statue of the Roman Emperor Constantine, in front of the Minster.

16. York Minster

The final destination on our city centre ghost walk is the awe-inspiring gothic cathedral which dominates York: the Minster. It truly is the crowning glory of the North of England, containing half the medieval

The Bedern Archway

stained glass in the country and built over the remains of earlier Norman and Roman buildings. As you would expect, several ghosts have been associated with such an ancient site.

In the middle of the 19th century a memorable but tragic supernatural event took place in the Minster. A young lady was being shown around the interior of the cathedral by an older gentleman when a man stepped out from behind one of the monuments. He was dressed as an officer, in full navy uniform, and as he walked towards the young lady he whispered chillingly, "There is a future state."

With this the figure disappeared from sight, and the lady collapsed in distress. When she had recovered, the older gentleman asked her to elucidate the cause of her discomfort. The young lady explained that the naval officer was her brother, currently serving at sea, and before his latest voyage the two of them had made a pact that whoever died first would try and contact the other if there was an afterlife. She was convinced that the figure they had just seen in the Minster was his ghost, and that he had appeared in order to confirm the existence of life after death to his sister.

Indeed, a few days later they officially received the sad news that her brother had died at sea, at the exact time that his phantom had approached her in the great cathedral.

This report of a continued posthumous state brings us to the end of our city centre ghost walk on a positive note. Perhaps we all have a great deal to look forward to.

York Minster

Walk Two:

From the outskirts to the heart of York

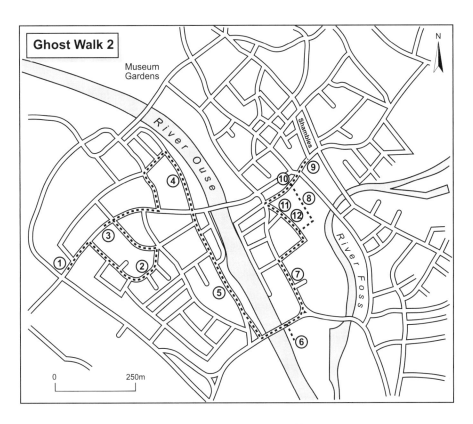

1. Micklegate Bar
2. Dance School
3. Holy Trinity, Micklegate
4. All Saints, North Street
5. Cock And Bottle
6. St. George's Field

7. Clifford's Tower
8. Body Shop
9. Golden Fleece
10. All Saints, Pavement
11. Little John
12. St. Mary's Church

This second walk around the haunted locations of York, begins at Mickelgate Bar, the imposing southern great gateway, through which countless monarchs have entered this beautiful, historical city. From its lofty battlements the decaying severed heads of traitors used to be displayed on spikes as a warning to the good citizens of York, to encourage them to remain good citizens of York.

From the city centre walk across Ouse Bridge and up the gentle incline to Micklegate Bar.

1. Micklegate Bar

This impressive portal is the southern entrance to the city, through which Kings and Queens passed, and for centuries the heads of traitors were displayed on spikes above its lofty battlements.

In 1797 Thomas Brocklebank was the gatekeeper and his family lived inside the building. His daughter, Sarah, decided to play a game with her brothers and sisters, hiding the keys to the Bar for them to find. Unfortunately, the keys were lost as the young girl could not remember where she had concealed them. This led to her father losing his job and the family being thrown out onto the streets.

A good deal of paranormal activity has been reported inside the Bar. Lights are switched on of their own accord, people feel the touch of tiny hands inside the building and a shadowy figure has been seen on the interior walls. It is thought that this can be attributed to the ghost of Sarah Brocklebank.

Electrical equipment sometimes malfunctions here and the presence of a spectral hound has made its presence known in the form of a distinctive 'wet dog' smell which comes and goes suddenly. The odour

Micklegate Bar

is thought to be connected to a long-haired dog which lived in the Bar with the last of its gatekeepers.

Continue along Micklegate and take the first turning on your right into Priory Street. At the end of Priory Street turn left into Bishophill Junior. Just around the corner, on your left is the McPherson School of Dancing.

2. Dance School

In the late 1960s reports emerged of inexplicable incidents in this hall, which was the home of a successful dance school. The building stands adjacent to the old church of St. Mary and indeed it was originally affiliated to it. Perhaps it was this ancient link that brought about the wealth of paranormal activity here: footsteps were repeatedly heard; locked exterior doors would be shaken aggressively by an invisible force; many small objects were levitated into the air or thrown across the hall and in the cellar one lady was physically pushed over by unseen hands.

Continue past the church and take the first turning on your left into Trinity Lane. At the end of this street, turn left back into Micklegate and shortly ahead on the left is the gateway of Holy Trinity Church.

The Dance School

3. Holy Trinity, Micklegate

In Victorian times there were many reports of three mysterious white figures which appeared on several occasions inside this church during daytime services. There was a tall young lady wearing a veil, another woman and an infant. In more recent years the woman in white has been seen from time to time in the churchyard, sometimes carrying a

Holy Trinity, Micklegate

baby in her arms, sometimes even running through the graveyard before vanishing.

It is believed that these ghosts go back to the Middle Ages and an outbreak of plague in the city, which took the life of a young widow's child. Although her husband had been interred in the grounds of this church, the infant had to be buried outside the city walls in order to prevent the spread of the pestilence. Upon her own death the woman was buried with her husband against her wishes: she had requested that her mortal remains should reside with those of her child. It is thought that the lady in white is seen looking for the infant she was separated from in death, sometimes even returning with her offspring to the churchyard.

Retrace your steps and continue downhill along Micklegate, towards the city centre, but take the second turning on the left into George

Hudson Street. Continue straight on and take the first turning on your right into Tanner Row. At the bottom of Tanner Row, turn right into North Street. Continue on past a small public garden on your left and on your right you will see All Saints Church.

4. All Saints, North Street

Perhaps because of its location on the far side of the Ouse, this impressive medieval church is often overlooked by visitors. Inside you will find exquisitely carved angels on the wooden ceiling and the fascinating 'Pricke of Conscience' stained-glass window depicting the last 15 days of the world as foretold in the *Book of Revelations* in *The Bible*. However, on this walk we are concerned with the exterior, as it is outside the front of the church that our next unexplained event occurred.

All Saints, North Street

On Christmas Eve 1953 a young man had arranged to meet his mother after she had attended midnight mass in this church. Across the road from the church is the little garden which you have just passed and as the young man arrived he noticed a lady sitting there whom he recognised since she was an old friend of his family. She came to the railings in front of the church and they exchanged festive greetings, before the man went to meet his mother as she came out of the church.

He thought nothing more of that encounter on Christmas Eve until the following January, when the family received the sad news that their old friend had in fact died the previous November. Yet somehow she had managed to wish them a Merry Christmas from beyond the grave.

The Cock And Bottle

Continue straight on, cross over Micklegate and go straight on into Skeldergate. A short distance ahead on your right is the Cock and Bottle.

5. The Cock And Bottle

A man in 17th century dress has been sighted inside this pub, suddenly appearing and departing. On one occasion the former landlady was having a shower upstairs, when the door of the bathroom opened and the figure walked in. He approached her and stood staring at the poor woman through the glass of her shower cubicle, before making his escape up some steps to an attic room. The landlady's screams brought her husband running in and, although they conducted a thorough search, no trace of the ghostly voyeur was found.

It is thought that this spectre may be George Villiers who enjoyed a hedonistic lifestyle during the reign of Charles II. His infatuation with the fairer sex is remembered in the nursery rhyme *Georgie Porgie* and it is said that his request to be buried in York was denied. Instead he was interred in Westminster Abbey. Clearly, it has not prevented him from revisiting this unforgettable city.

Continue straight on along Skeldergate and at the end of the street turn left onto Skeldergate Bridge. Walk along the bridge and go down the steps on your left. At the bottom of the steps, turn left under the bridge. You are now standing on a tree-lined path, St. George's Field.

6. St. George's Field

A spectral rider has been seen racing down this riverside pathway, hurtling past the trees on the back of a horse. His dark clothes are typical of the 18th century and he wears a distinctive tricorn hat. Popular tradition has identified this ghostly horseman as the brutal highwayman Dick Turpin, who met his end in York in 1739, although the identity of the phantom rider has yet to be clearly established. Glance down the pathway and imagine the sight of the dark rider approaching on his horse, its hooves thundering on the ground. Is this

St. George's Field

figure's hasty flight a replay from a forgotten incident in York's long history?

Retrace your steps back under the bridge and up the steps, turn left then follow the road round to the left as it turns into Tower Street. Cross over the road and Clifford's Tower is ahead on your right.

7. Clifford's Tower

One of the most impressive land marks in the city, Clifford's Tower is the keep and main surviving section of York Castle, the walls of which used to surround the area now occupied by the excellent Castle Museum. The tower was originally built of wood and was constructed on the orders of William the Conqueror in 1068, in the wake of his success at the battle of Hastings.

It is in this original wooden tower that the appalling events of our next story took place in 1190. Many citizens of York owed money to members of the Jewish community and the Jews became targets of propaganda and hatred. One evening a riot began on the streets and it soon escalated into an angry mob intent on seeking out and attacking all the Jews they could find. Believing they were under the protection of King Richard I, the Jewish community sought safety inside the walls of York Castle, but the mob followed and besieged them there. In utter despair, realising they would not be allowed to get out alive, the Jews burnt their possessions then each man cut the throat of his wife and children before killing himself, resulting in a horrific death toll of 150 innocent people.

Since that time many people have reported unusual red colourations on the stones and floor of Clifford's tower and visiting children have actually seen crimson blood running down the outer walls of the

Clifford's Tower

building. It seems that the traumatic events of that night so long ago still manifest themselves in our current century.

Follow Tower Street round to the right, with the tower itself always on your right, then turn left into Castlegate. Shortly ahead turn right past the church and into the pedestrianised St. Mary's Square. Turn left and continue straight on, passing the ever-popular Jorvik Viking Centre on your left as you walk up the slight incline of Coppergate Walk. The Body Shop is on your right.

8. The Body Shop

Shortly after the redevelopment of Coppergate in the 1980s staff at this branch of the Body Shop started to have strange experiences in the store; indeed at the time their accounts of poltergeist activity here

The Body Shop

were even featured on television. One evening, long after the shop had been locked up for the night, the glass front of the fire alarm was smashed. Fire engines raced to the building, only to find it still locked and empty. The glass was replaced yet the alarm was set off twice more during the same night. The invisible force at work was obviously having fun.

The Body Shop and the surrounding stores were built on the site of Craven's Sweet factory, which for years was plagued by a poltergeist. It seems that the spirit has survived the demolition of its original haunt.

This ghost may have a connection to a woman who lived in a house in this area, opposite All Saints church. Her personality was considered wicked, mean and dishonest. On her deathbed she cursed her demise and swore to return. Her old house was plagued by disturbing noises and no-one could bear to stay in the dark bedroom in which she had died. Could this be the restless spirit which now makes its presence known in the Body Shop?

Continue straight on then turn right into Coppergate. Go straight on into Pavement. The Golden Fleece is ahead on your right, opposite the bottom entrance to York's most magical medieval street, the Shambles.

9. The Golden Fleece

This historical inn is renowned for its many ghosts including the mischievous spirit of a young Victorian boy whose small hands are felt going into people's pockets. He is also believed to be responsible for the movement of small objects which are seen to fly off the tables and smash into the wall. Other phenomena include doors opening and closing by themselves, glasses moving, unexpected drops in temperature, strange footsteps on the stairs and taps turning themselves on.

Visitors have seen the ghost of a World War II Canadian airman upstairs, still in his distinctive uniform. It is believed that the unfortunate man hanged himself in one of the bedrooms after hearing

The Golden Fleece

of his wife's infidelity. He still wanders across the room and vanishes into the wall.

Retrace your path back along Pavement and Coppergate. Stop at the top of Coppergate Walk; All Saints Church is across the road.

10. All Saints, Pavement

A beautiful long-haired lady in a white dress was seen around this church several times. She would regularly appear during the daytime at funeral services and had a sympathetic demeanour, welcoming the mourners into the church. In recent years this spirit has been less active, but like so many of the ghosts reported there was nothing transparent or insubstantial about her. Indeed she was described as radiant and looked just as healthy and real as a living person until she vanished suddenly.

All Saints, Pavement

Continue along Coppergate then turn left into Castlegate. Ahead on your left is The Little John.

11. The Little John

The Little John

We cannot pass this fine pub without mentioning its gruesome place in York's history. For, after being hanged at the Knavesmire (now York's racecourse), the body of the notorious highwayman Dick Turpin was laid out in the cellar of this alehouse in 1739. In a macabre display of their fascination with the brutal criminal, the people of York queued up to pay a penny each to view the corpse.

Continue along Castlegate a short distance; St. Mary's Church is on your left.

12. St. Mary's Church

In the 1970s the BBC broadcast a programme investigating people's ability to recall past lives under hypnosis. Arnall Bloxham had carried out hundreds of these regressions, recording the sessions onto tape. One of his subjects recalled a former existence as a Jewish girl named Rebecca in York during 1189-90. She recounted that she was present at the dreadful siege in Clifford's Tower, but that she fled from the castle seeking a safe haven in the crypt of a nearby church along with her daughter. Unfortunately, her escape was in vain and the two Jewesses were soon discovered and brutally murdered by the mob.

This tale was initially rejected as fiction by local historians who knew that, apart from the Minster, there was no church containing a crypt at that time in York. Events took a fascinating turn, however, when in 1975 (long after the regression recording had been made) workmen were renovating St. Mary's church. Under its floor they discovered the

St. Mary's Church

concealed remains of a subterranean stone chamber belonging to an earlier church on the same site. Was this the crypt recalled by Rebecca? How could a lady in the twentieth century know of such a room when historical experts were ignorant of its existence?

On this intriguing but promising thought, we end our second ghost walk through York, in my opinion the finest and most haunted city in the world.

Walk Three:

Around the haunted walls

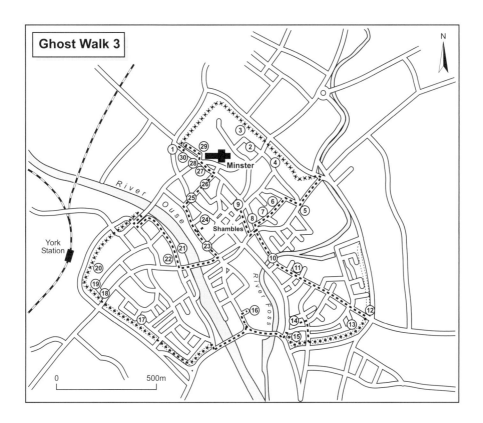

1. Bootham Bar
2. York Minster
3. Treasurer's House
4. Bedern
5. The Black Swan
6. Lady Hewley's Hospital
7. St. Saviour's Church
8. St. Crux
9. The Shambles
10. The Foss Bridge
11. The Five Lions
12. Walmgate Bar
13. York Minster
14. Dick Turpin's Grave
15. The Castle Museum
16. Clifford's Tower
17. St. Mary's Church
18. Micklegate Bar
19. The Windmill
20. York Railway Station
21. The Park Inn Hotel
22. The Yorkshire Hussar
23. Boots
24. Judge's Court
25. The Punch Bowl
26. Coffee Yard
27. The Dean Court Hotel
28. The York Arms
29. Precentor's Court
30. The Hole in the Wall

Our third and longest walk will take us onto and around the impressive medieval city walls of York. This outing must take place during daylight hours as the walls are closed at dusk but this is fortunate as so much of York's ghostly history can be seen from these ancient ramparts. We begin in Exhibition Square at Bootham Bar, one of the four impressive stone entrances into the walled city.

Bootham Bar stands on the site of a former Roman gateway into the fortress of Eboracum so people have been entering and leaving at this point for almost two thousand years. Perhaps it is unsurprising that so many souls, so many lives, have left an impression on York's unique atmosphere.

1. Bootham Bar

Ascend the steps into the guardroom then look out of the arrow-slits on the right, down into the street below. You will be able to see the historical Hole in the Wall public house.

One of the old houses between the Hole in the Wall and Bootham Bar was formerly a hairdresser's shop. The owner's family lived above the shop and on several occasions at night after closing time they heard the sound of the locked front door being opened and the bell ringing. Footsteps would then be heard climbing the stairs before the chilling noise faded away. Afterwards, the door was always found to still be locked and nobody could be seen on the stairs.

Also in this area, on a sunny day in the early nineteen seventies, a lady had just walked through Bootham Bar, heading towards the Minster, when she clearly saw a nun in a brown faded habit with a white collar. The nun continued towards Bootham Bar before disappearing. The description of the habit did not match any in use at the time, but rather belonged to a much earlier period.

Leave the guardhouse through the doorway onto the ramparts. This is surely the most charming and picturesque section of the walls and almost immediately on the right we see the impressive towers of the Minster.

Bootham Bar

2. York Minster

In the late 1960s the Minster was undergoing essential renovation work to strengthen its foundations after a structural survey revealed that the central tower was near to collapse. A lady who visited the cathedral at that time became aware of a small, roughly dressed man standing beside her as she was looking up and admiring the architecture on the ceiling. He pointed at one of the wooden bosses and told her "I carved that" before fading away into thin air. Perhaps this apparition of a medieval workman had been brought into existence by the disturbance to the fabric of the great

York Minster, viewed from the city walls

building, as often seems to happen when structural alterations are made to historical sites.

Continue along the walls and follow the walkway as it turns right at the corner. From Bootham Bar we have been walking along the layout of the original Roman walls and, shortly after a green plaque on the left, we soon see the back of the Treasurer's House.

3. Treasurer's House

The ghostly legion of Roman soldiers witnessed by Harry Martindale in the cellar of this fine building appeared to be travelling along the former *Via Decumana*, the Roman road which Chapter House street approximates today. However, the Roman road would have continued and joined the wall at a gateway which used to exist very close to where you are now standing. The Roman soldiers, though, are not the only spirits haunting the magnificent Treasurer's House.

For many years visitors noticed that the ornate, wood-paneled Tapestry Room always felt colder than the rest of the house and seemed to have an oppressive atmosphere. It transpired that at some point in the building's long history some of the rooms were divided up and rented out as separate accommodation and the Tapestry Room was occupied by a married couple. It seems that the husband was often unfaithful and even went so far as to suggest to his long-suffering wife that his mistress should move in with them. Soon afterwards, the outraged woman stabbed him to death in the room bringing matters to a disturbing conclusion.

The back of the Treasurer's House

A few years ago, a young girl visiting the Treasurer's House sat on a large antique chair in the Tapestry Room, telling her surprised parents that she was sitting next to a lady she could see. Was this female figure, invisible to the adults, the ghost of the wronged wife from so long ago?

Continue along the walls and go down the steps when you reach them. You are now at the back of another great gateway, Monk Bar. Near here the sound of ghostly chains being rattled in the dead of night have been heard on many occasions. Cross the road and ascend the steps on the other side of the Bar onto the next section of walls. A short distance ahead on the right is the timber-framed Merchant Taylors' Hall. Stop just before this impressive building and look down the street to your right. The majority of the buildings of Bedern are modern yet it is still one of the most haunted areas in York.

4. Bedern

In Walk One we included the sad tale of the children neglected in the York Industrial Ragged School during Victorian times and how they continue to make their presence known today. An archaeologist working with a trowel in this area repeatedly felt someone tapping him on the back, but each time he turned around there was nobody there. That night, when he went to bed, his wife noticed several scratch marks down his back, as if he'd been scraped by little fingers.

Residents in the new houses have reported children's shadows on the walls and others have seen children in Victorian dress in the new square. Several people have felt tiny, invisible hands slip into theirs as they walk through these streets and even felt someone blow in their ear. Despite their terrible end, these youthful spirits seem to have retained their childish playfulness.

Continue along the walls; shortly after the walkway turns to the left, go down the steps and through the stone archway onto the pavement. Continue around the corner to your right and straight on past the church. To your left, across the road, is the Black Swan public house.

Bedern, seen from the walls

5. The Black Swan

This fine medieval timber-framed pub is haunted by at least three spectres. A young woman in a long, white dress walks through the bar and stands looking down into the fire. Her long, black hair conceals her features. A Victorian man in a bowler hat walks impatiently through the rooms and tuts, as if irritated by someone's failure to arrive, before vanishing. Most unusually just a pair of legs, belonging to a man, have been seen walking around the landlord's quarters.

Immediately opposite the Black Swan are two streets; take the one on the left, then turn left into St. Saviourgate. Halfway down the street, on the left, is a stone building with an impressive coat of arms and an inscription concerning the founding of the Hewley Hospital.

The Black Swan

6. Lady Hewley's Hospital

About two hundred years ago a large, abandoned house stood in the spot now occupied by this fine building. It lay empty for many years and had the reputation of being haunted by a beautiful woman with long hair. She was thought to appear at the door of the house when the church clock struck midnight and could be observed walking past the graveyard to stand outside the church. She would pace up and down, as though awaiting someone, until the bell chimed one and then the ghostly figure would walk back to the door of the derelict house. No explanation was ever discovered for the apparition but this activity seems to have ended with the demolition of the empty house and the hospital's construction in 1840.

Lady Hewley's Hospital

A short distance ahead on the left is St. Saviour's Church.

7. St. Saviour's Church

Now the home of York's educational archaeological attraction 'Dig', this age-old church has also been the location for the restless poltergeist activity of a malevolent spirit. It is believed that this may be the disturbed ghost of a Viking warrior who was tied to the church door and skinned alive by York's Christian residents.

Another disturbing incident occurred during Victorian times in the church's graveyard. One wealthy lady had recently been buried in a vault, still wearing her expensive jewellery. A gravedigger of the parish returned to the eerie churchyard at night, using the cover of darkness

St.Saviour's Church

to conceal his grizzly theft of the valuables. He re-opened the vault, lifted open the lid of the coffin and started to take the rings from the fingers of the corpse. One ring was stuck, however, so the callous gravedigger took out a knife and began to cut into one of the deceased's fingers. At this point the corpse of the dead woman started to move and moan, terrifying the shocked thief who fled from the scene.

It seems that the rich lady had not been dead at all, merely in a coma. The pain of the cut and the flow of blood had returned her to consciousness. In fact she made a total recovery. For once dishonourable intentions brought about a positive outcome.

At night, the form of a man in a top hat has been seen among the gravestones of this church. Once his presence has been detected by passers-by, the figure rushes away. Could this be the shade of the gravedigger still seeking his ill-gotten gains amongst the dead?

Continue to the end of St. Saviourgate, cross the road and bear left towards the stone building on the corner of the intriguingly-named Whip-Ma-Whop-Ma-Gate.

8. St. Crux

The remains of this church still stand at the bottom of the Shambles, although the main building was demolished in 1887. The ghost of a tall man was often glimpsed here in the early hours of the morning by cleaning ladies walking past on their way to work. The man would stand at the windows and stare down into the street, never leaving the church.

The second ghost associated with the church was a beautiful lady in white who was seen during the winter emerging from the churchyard and walking as far as Goodramgate before vanishing.

Another intriguing account concerns a policeman who was passing St. Crux late one night when he distinctly heard loud funeral music being played on the church organ. As if this wasn't alarming enough the

Whip-Ma-Whop-Ma-Gate with the stone walls of St.Crux behind

church door slowly opened and he heard the sound of the congregation leaving, even though he could see nobody there. In fact, he even felt the fabric of dresses brush against his legs as the invisible mourners went by. Then the church door closed and the area fell silent again.

Follow the pavement round to the right into the Shambles.

9. The Shambles

York's most famous historical street once housed the city's butchers' shops and is home to at least one ghost. When the Shambles falls quiet late in the evening, as you wander down the narrow road past the crowded together timber-framed houses it is extremely atmospheric and the perfect setting for a typical ghost story. Fittingly enough it is a headless figure who is seen late at night stumbling over the cobble stones, searching in vain for his lost head and dressed in garments from centuries ago. Many believe this to be the same phantom who frequents the graveyard of Holy Trinity church, Thomas Percy.

At the bottom of the Shambles cross over Pavement and bear left, then take the next turning on your right into Fossgate. Continue

The Shambles

straight on, past the beautifully decorated entrance to the Merchant Adventurers' Hall and after a short distance you will be standing on the Foss Bridge.

10. Foss Bridge

A lady in a shroud has been seen walking from the bottom of the Shambles down to this bridge, where she disappears. This may be the same ghost that was known to walk from St. Crux church up to Goodramgate, then vanish. She was known to be fond of the tunes played by the Waits of York, men who were paid to perform music in the streets. The ghostly lady in white would walk behind the musicians through the streets.

Continue straight ahead into Walmgate and on your left is the Five Lions public house.

The Foss Bridge

11. Five Lions

This interesting pub originally had an extra floor with a long, narrow room where cock fights were once held. It also has a ghost known as Green Jenny. Little is known about her but at the start of the last century she passed a man on the back stairs before vanishing in front of his eyes. Since that time strange shadows have been seen on the stairs.

The Five Lions

Go straight on until you can see the reassuring towers of Walmgate Bar, the only great gateway in York to have retained its impressive barbican. Ascend the steps to the right of the Bar.

12. Walmgate Bar

In this area the ghost of a Labrador dog has been seen on the walls. It seems the poor animal was the victim of a group of heartless troublemakers who pushed the creature off the walls into the path of an oncoming lorry. The phantom canine now patrols the ramparts.

Walmgate Bar

Continue along the walls and on the right, above the rooftops, we soon catch sight of York Minster, always at the heart of this great city.

13. York Minster

As you would expect, this great cathedral has been the setting for many ghost sightings. Dean Gale, who used to work in the Minster and died in 1702, has been glimpsed sitting at his habitual pew, still listening to the church services inside. A monk has been seen to wander up and down the centre aisle and a man in a white Elizabethan costume has appeared. A phantom dog has also been heard on several occasions after the animal was bricked up in a wall by some callous workmen building the cathedral, and left to die.

Continue along the walls until you descend the next steps to ground level then turn right towards St. George's Church, which was once plagued by a ghostly rabbit running up and down its aisles at night, then cross Lead Mill Lane and shortly afterwards turn left into the graveyard.

York Minster, towering above the rooftops

14. St. George's Church Graveyard

This is Dick Turpin's final resting place – his is the large grave towards the back. A notorious horse thief, house breaker and murderer, the real Turpin was not a dashing gentleman of the road. He was hanged at the Knavesmire (now York racecourse) in 1739. A few years ago on the A64 road between York and Malton, a driver was passing the Four Alls public house shortly before midnight. He clearly saw a man on horseback dressed in highwayman's clothing and wearing a tricorn hat outside the pub. He looked back again in his rear-view mirror but the highwayman had disappeared. Could this have been the ghost of Dick Turpin?

Dick Turpin's Grave

Retrace your path back to the city walls and go up the steps on the right. Continue along the walls until you reach the corner where the pathway turns to the right. Stop and look out over the walls. To your right you will see part of the Castle Museum.

15. Castle Museum

This brilliant museum is formed from former prison buildings and in fact Dick Turpin spent his last night alive here in the condemned cell. It is perhaps not surprising, then, that strange sounds have been heard here including disembodied muttering, scratching noises and a female voice singing a lullaby. A ghostly dog has been sighted and an elderly woman dressed in black has also appeared sitting in front of a fireplace.

The Castle Museum

Continue along the walls then descend the steps to ground level. Cross over Piccadilly and carry straight on over the bridge. Follow the pavement round to the right and on your right is the imposing stone edifice of Clifford's Tower.

16. The Barguest

Clifford's Tower, haunt of the York Barquest?

Stories about the Barguest, a huge, black ghostly dog, have been told for centuries in York. Sightings of the fierce, spectral hell hound have been reported on the walls and here at Clifford's Tower. This particular canine is far from being a man's best friend, however. For those unfortunate enough to see the creature, it is said to be an omen of impending doom.

Cross over Tower Street at the pedestrian crossing, then turn left and follow the pavement round to the right and over Skeldergate bridge. Then cross Skeldergate and ascend the steps to rejoin the city walls. Follow the walls ahead, then around the corner to the right and straight on. Immediately after passing a children's play area, look up the street to the right and you will see the stone tower of St. Mary's Church.

17. St. Mary's Church

This is one of York's oldest churches and so perhaps it is not surprising that there is a great deal of ghostly activity connected to it. The building next to the church once had an ecclesiastical use and it seems that sounds from the past are replayed inside. One eerie sequence heard again and again was the noise of coins being emptied onto a table and counted, then dropped into a chest. The chilling sound of the money would grow louder and louder until the lid of the chest was heard to slam shut. Was this the priest of St. Mary's counting the collection from his church? Could the noise still be audible centuries later and replayed time and time again, unnerving York's present residents?

Continue along the walls and you will soon reach Micklegate Bar. Descend the steps, cross the road and go up the steps on the other side.

St.Mary's Church Tower

18. Micklegate Bar

Micklegate Bar, seen from the walls

In the early 1970s a lady had just ascended these steps and was about four metres from Micklegate Bar when suddenly an icy feeling of terror gripped her. She was utterly horrified and her fear prevented her from moving from the spot. Then, as she looked along the walls, she saw the lower half of a friar: sandals, legs and black robes. The figure spoke to her, "Do not be afraid. Follow me!" She followed her ghostly rescuer a short distance along the walls, now feeling greatly reassured, and then the insubstantial friar vanished. The lady believed that she had been attacked by a negative entity before the ghostly monk came to her aid.

Go forward a short distance then look back over your left shoulder, down towards the crossroads in front of Micklegate Bar. The Windmill public house is on the nearest corner, opposite the building with pillars.

19. The Windmill

Another of York's many haunted pubs, this inn has been the location of several paranormal anomalies over the years. Icy cold mists have appeared inside the building, glasses and bottles have been moved or shattered, ghostly footsteps have been heard on the stairs and, in cellars and storerooms, lights have been switched on overnight. It is also said that this pub is haunted by the spirit of a young girl who was tragically run over and killed by a brewer's cart many decades ago.

The Windmill

Continue along the walls and, after the walkway turns to the right, look to your left and you will see York's splendid railway station. Just behind the station, in Leeman Road, is the excellent National Railway Museum.

20. National Railway Museum

Unearthly voices have been heard as well as ghostly footsteps walking between the many locomotives. A spectral figure has been observed walking around the empty carriages, some of which date back to Victorian times.

In recent years, much interest has, surprisingly, been generated online by the pedestrian tunnel outside the National Railway Museum. A mobile phone video was posted on the internet, taken by two young women as they returned home via the tunnel after a night out on the town. The video claimed to show the two young ladies being menaced by a 'leering ghost', although the picture quality was quite poor. After the girls had walked through approximately half the length of the tunnel, a white skull-like shape was visible behind one of them and it appeared to follow the two revellers as they ran outside. Opinion

York Railway Station. The National Railway Museum is in nearby Leeman Road

online was divided as to whether the 'ghost' was genuine or merely a visual anomaly, produced by a combination of the tunnel's lighting and the mobile phone's low image resolution. It will be interesting to see whether any more experiences of this nature occur in the Leeman Road tunnel in the future.

Continue straight on along the walls until they come down to pavement level just before Lendal Bridge. Instead of crossing the bridge, continue downhill on the pavement to your right to the pedestrian crossing; then cross over into Tanner's Moat. Go straight on towards the river, to the end of Tanner's Moat, then turn right into Wellington Row. Continue straight on into North Street where, just ahead on the left, is the Park Inn Hotel.

21. Park Inn Hotel

The Park Inn Hotel

This is a relatively modern building, but its ghost is apparently connected to the row of houses which previously stood here. A murder was carried out in one of the houses a long time ago and it was believed to be haunted. There have been several reports of a shadowy, vague shape on the hotel stairs indicating that ghosts do not always disappear when buildings are demolished. In fact, building work often seems to lead to an increase in paranormal activity.

Opposite the Park Inn Hotel is the Yorkshire Hussar public house.

22. Yorkshire Hussar

The Yorkshire Hussar

Late one evening four painters and decorators were working through the night to complete a job in this pub. They were disturbed to see a man in a cape who walked past them and disappeared into one of the walls behind the bar, where a door had previously been. Bar stools have also been knocked over and glasses smashed by invisible hands.

Continue straight on and, at the end of North Street, turn left into Bridge Street and go over Ouse Bridge. Across the bridge, turn left into Spurriergate and go straight on. Ahead on the left is the Boots store.

23. Boots

The site currently occupied by Boots once housed a large Elizabethan mansion which was regularly used to accommodate judges staying in York for the assizes, periodic criminal courts held from time to time. In the first years of the 19th century two lawyers stayed in the dark, timber-framed building during November in a large second-floor room. Having arrived late in the evening and tired from their journey, they soon fell asleep in their beds. In the middle of the night, however, one man awoke feeling cold and strangely frightened. In the darkness he heard footsteps, then the sound of a struggle, a scream and the noise of someone falling to the floor heavily. He lit a candle only to find that there was nobody else there except his colleague and that the door of their room was still bolted on the inside.

The next morning the terrified lawyer spoke to the housekeeper about his strange experience. The lady was not surprised by his story as it transpired that others had heard similar noises of a scuffle in the same room.

She went on to explain that a hundred years earlier one particular judge, a cruel and ruthless man, was staying in the house with his young nephew. One night the noise of a struggle was heard from their second-floor room and when servants went to investigate, the poor youth was found lying on the floor dead, having been stabbed through the chest.

However, despite the appalling act of murder which he had committed, there was to be no punishment for this particular brutal judge. On account of his social standing the judge's killing was

Boots

covered up and the death was treated as suicide. Yet the ghostly sounds of the terrible murder were still filling the air of that dark chamber a century after the murderer had escaped justice.

Continue straight ahead along Spurriergate and, before you reach the ruined church on the left, look for a passageway on your right identified as 'Judge's Court'. Walk down the gloomy passage into the small courtyard.

24. Judge's Court

The ghost of a large man in black has been reported here and his footsteps have been heard on the stairs of the building in front of you since the early years of the 20th century. The steps were quite distinctive as they were always accompanied by a metallic tinkling sound.

Years later, when some renovation work was being conducted here, a skeleton was discovered at the bottom of a disused well. The bones belonged to heavily-built man and about the feet were remnants of his riding boots with one broken spur. It is thought that this may explain the metallic jangling noise heard between the ghostly footsteps.

Judge's Court

Retrace your steps back along the passageway, then turn right into Coney Street. You soon come to the picturesque St. Helen's Square; cross the Square and enter Stonegate. A short distance ahead on your right is the Punch Bowl public house.

25. The Punch Bowl

This fine timber-framed building is home to at least two ghosts. A few hundred years ago it was apparently also a house of ill repute and one ruffian pursued a terrified woman through the upper rooms before finally strangling her to death. Customers still hear her desperate footsteps coming from the ceiling as they enjoy a drink in the bar.

Many years ago one unfortunate landlord was burnt to death in a fire here and his disembodied footsteps are still heard going down to the cellar. The cellar roof was later lowered to a height of five feet and a spherical glowing light, said to be the landlord's head, has been seen moving across the floor in the bar in the area above the cellar. Perhaps the unhappy publican still wanders through his inn, obliviously carrying out the daily routine *ad infinitum.*

Continue along Stonegate, noticing the many alleyways which lead away from this historic thoroughfare. One of them was formerly known as Church Passage.

The Punch Bowl

26. Curch Passage

There used to be a few houses down this alley and, at the time of the First World War, one of them was home to a lady and her young daughter. With the husband away in the army, the woman and girl were alarmed to hear regular ghostly noises in the house. At about ten o'clock each night there would be the sound of a person entering the hallway and taking off a coat, then eerie footsteps would go up the stairs although there was nobody to be seen. After a while there would be a loud, unnerving crash as though something was thrown to the floor upstairs. The sources of the strange noises were never explained.

Coffee Yard, one of the many alleyways leading from Stonegate

Continue to the top of Stonegate, turn left into High Petergate and carry on until the junction with Duncombe Place. The Dean Court Hotel is across the road.

27. Dean Court Hotel

The Dean Court Hotel

This fine building must surely be the best placed hotel in York, situated so close to the Minster. One of its rooms was the location for an intriguing experience for three guests who all saw a Roman soldier in a bathroom mirror. Indeed, this ancient apparition has been known to wander through several rooms. The Roman fortress of *Eboracum* had its headquarters where the Minster now stands and so it is perhaps unsurprising that there have been other sightings of Roman soldiers across this area of York.

Cross Duncombe Place and continue along High Petergate for a short distance. The York Arms public house is on your right.

28. York Arms

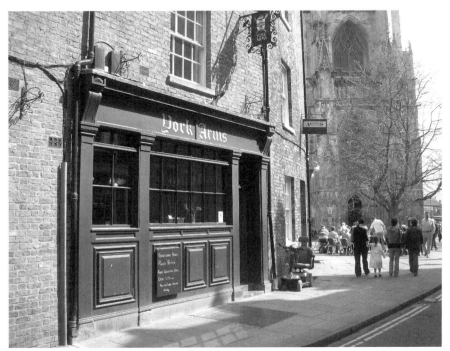

The York Arms

A grey lady in flowing garments has been seen on the stairs here on several occasions. Some believe her to be the ghost of a nun from centuries ago. She certainly gave one male customer the fright of his life when she appeared in front of him in the gentlemen's toilet!

Other unusual occurrences include doors opening and closing by themselves and objects being moved around or thrown. Someone or something is clearly trying to make its presence known.

Cross High Petergate and head back towards the Minster. Turn the corner and bear left into the secluded Precentor's Court.

29. Precentor's Court

This charming cul-de-sac, with its magnificent and unexpected view of the Minster, was the setting for a paranormal event many years ago. On a dark winter's evening a young woman came to visit her friends who lived in one of the houses here. Although no lights were on, she knocked at the front door repeatedly, thinking her friends might be in a room at the back. Eventually, the door opened and standing at the threshold was a boy she did not recognise. He was bathed in a strange, eerie glow which gradually increased to illuminate the whole doorway.

In terror, the woman ran to other acquaintances who lived nearby and related her disturbing experience. The men of the house returned to Precentor's Court but found that the front door was now locked and in complete darkness. In fact, it transpired that the owners had been

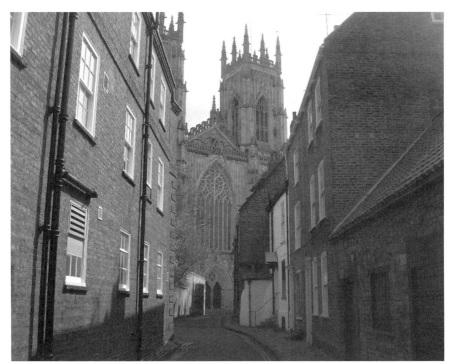

The Minister, viewed from Precentor's Court

absent for over a month and no normal explanation for the glowing child could be found.

Continue along Precentor's Court to the end, then turn left along the alleyway and onto the pavement beyond. You are now standing outside the Hole in the Wall public house.

30. Hole in the Wall

In 1816 secret dungeons were discovered in this historic building, including a cavity in one of the walls which still contained rusty chains and manacles. This is the origin of the pub's unusual name; it was formerly known as the Board Inn. Intriguingly, age-old rumours tell of a secret tunnel from its cellar to the Minster but no trace of it has ever been uncovered.

The Hole in the Wall

Strange, white mists have materialised in the bar, as has a man who mysteriously vanished. The ghost of a woman was seen upstairs. Who knows what past terrors were endured in this inn? It is perhaps understandable that the traumas of centuries ago have left their mark on the present.

From the Hole in the Wall you will see the reassuring lofty towers of Bootham Bar. We have come full circle and find ourselves back at our starting point in this ancient and fascinating city. Our eerie odyssey is at an end.

But is York
really haunted?

Despite the huge body of evidence that unusual events do occur in York, a wander through the lovely streets on a beautiful sunny day may cause you to side with the sceptics. It's so peaceful and reassuring in its historic splendour that you may quite rationally refuse to believe a word of the stories in this book until you encounter the paranormal for yourself. I can't promise that you will, although I can add my own account from personal experience of an unnerving and inexplicable event one night in York.

In May 1989 my wife, Janet, and I had rented a first floor flat in Holgate Road for a week's break in our favourite city. We had stayed in the same flat the previous year, without incident, but on this occasion as we arrived on the Saturday afternoon and were met by the landlord he happened to mention that the two elderly ladies who had been in the house the week before had cut their stay short, explaining that it was 'because of the noise'. We naturally assumed that this meant the traffic outside on the fairly busy road.

All went well during the first part of the week and we spent pleasant days immersed in the history and charms of York, walking the walls and visiting the excellent museums in town. However, on the Thursday night we were reading by the light of bedside lamps when we began to hear a slow, repeated, loud dull thud. At first we both ignored the noise, not wishing to acknowledge to each other that it was there, because we knew that we were in the only one of the three flats in the house to be occupied. The noise grew louder and was unmistakably inside our building: it was coming from the staircase between the ground and first floor. An ominous, repeated loud thump. It sounded as if something was being dragged down the stairs, banging loudly on each step.

As the noise continued we reluctantly had to admit to each other that we were both very aware of it. We got out of bed and headed to the door of the flat which led onto the landing, not knowing what to do but thoroughly terrified. I urged caution, believing that we were at least safer behind the locked door of the flat, but my wife insisted on getting to the bottom of the mystery. We unlocked the flat's door and stepped onto the landing frightened out of our wits, then turned on the light to illuminate the stairs.

The noise stopped. There was nothing there. Janet wanted to investigate further, so I bravely (!) volunteered to operate the light switch (which would turn itself off on a short timer unless repeatedly pushed) while she walked down the now-silent steps and checked the front door, which was still locked, exactly as we had left it earlier in the evening.

Fortunately, that was the last we heard of the eerie noise. The rest of the night was quiet and we spent the Friday night in the flat (after first fortifying ourselves with a visit to the pub across the road) without any further disturbance. We can offer no natural explanation for the loud, terrifying thuds we heard within those walls. The sound was at such a high volume that it could not have come from a neighbouring property, and as it happened the stairs of the property next door were not next to ours. We were the only people in the house that week and the doors were locked.

It was only later that we remembered the two old ladies who had left unexpectedly in the middle of the previous week 'because of the noise'...

If, like myself, you have come to believe that many people over the years have genuinely experienced paranormal and unexplained events in York, the question is what exactly are they? Are we seeing or hearing some kind of playback from years gone by, somehow recorded in the fabric of the buildings and triggered by atmospheric conditions? Can we attribute it to our senses being deceived by our brains in some way? Or could the spirits of our dead predecessors really return to visit the places they have known in life? Perhaps time will tell, perhaps at a future date science will advance to a point where we will be able to rationalise such extraordinary experiences. Until then we will have to be content in reading these amazing accounts and acknowledging York's well-deserved reputation as the world's most haunted city.

More books from Sigma Press

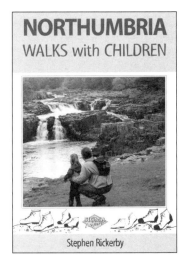

Northumbria Walks with Children
Stephen Rickerby

Over 20 walks are included covering the North East from the Tees to the Tweed. There are questions (with answers!) and checklists to both challenge and interest the children, as well as practical information for parents. All walks are less than 5 miles long, exploring the great variety of scenery and heritage of Northumbria.
'This is a splendid collection that will excite and stimulate youngsters.'
– Sunderland Echo

£7.95

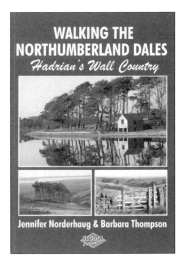

Walking The Northumberland Dales
Hadrian's Wall Country
Barbara Thompson

Explore the landscapes of North and South Tynedale, Allendale, Hexhamshire, Blanchland and Hadrian's Wall. The walks are packed with interest on the history, industrial archeology and the area's traditions, and culture.

£8.95

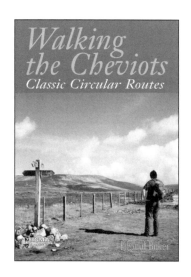

Walking the Cheviots
Classic Circular Routes
Edward Baker

The walks in this book provide an excellent introduction to this lonely, wild countryside — a true wilderness area. Everyone is catered for — from weekend family groups to the experienced hill walker. Each route is full of interest, with details of the natural history, geology and archaeology of the area.

£9.95

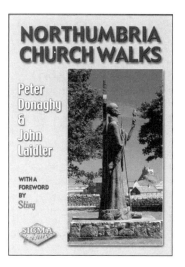

Northumbria Church Walks
Peter Donaghy & John Laidler
With a Foreword by Sting

30 circular walks, from 4 to 12 miles with alternative shorter options, combined with over 40 churches open to visitors with fine examples of stained glass, ancient crosses, medieval fonts, carvings and sculptures.

£8.95

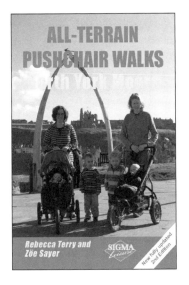

All-Terrain Pushchair Walks
The North York Moors
Zoë Sayer and Rebecca Terry

Explore the North York Moors — the perfect place to both keep fit and introduce your children to the delights of the outdoors. This fully revised and updated 2nd edition includes gradings and at-a-glance symbols to make walk choice easy and allow you to plan ahead. There are 30 walks spread across the entire national park from riverside walks and coastal strolls to rambles through the heather moors.

£8.99

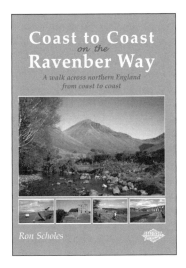

Coast to Coast
On the Ravenber Way
Ron Scholes

The walk described in the book follows existing rights of way in the form of footpaths, bridleways and tracks, making this cross-country route a challenging long-distance journey. The walk commences at Ravenglass, it passes Lakeland's finest array of high peaks, climbs over the high Pennines, traverses the northern moors and ends at Berwick-upon-Tweed.

£8.99

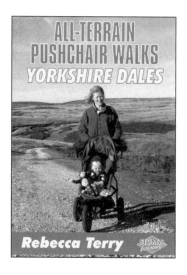

All-Terrain Pushchair Walks: Yorkshire Dales
Rebecca Terry

Find out the best of what the Yorkshire Dales has to offer with these 30 tried and tested all-terrain pushchair walks through open moorland and country estates, and alongside the beautiful and dramatic rivers for which this National Park is renowned. The walks are all accurately graded and have at-a-glance symbols making choosing easier.

£8.99

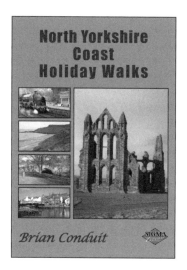

North Yorkshire Coast Holiday Walks
Brian Conduit

With its glorious sandy beaches and spectacular scenery, the North Yorkshire coast has long been a favourite holiday destination. The 20 walks range from 2½ to 6½ miles, a well as varying in length, they vary in difficulty and the nature of the terrain and some are inevitably more strenuous and involve more hill climbing than others.

£8.99

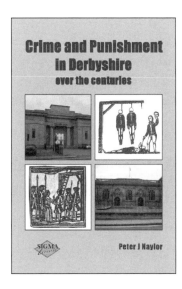

Derbyshire Crime
Over the centuries
Peter J Naylor

Crime fascinates us all, particularly murders, and the bloodier they are the better they are received. It would appear that the Peak District was a lawless place until more recent times. This book is a thorough mix of most of the types of crimes committed in Derbyshire over the centuries. Each chapter is dedicated to a different type of crime and the punishments handed out.

£8.99

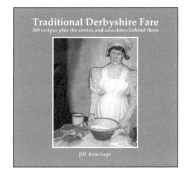

Traditional Derbyshire Fare
300 recipes plus the stories and anecdotes behind them
Jill Armitage

Some Derbyshire dishes, like the Bakewell Pudding, are well known; many more, including some of the most delectable, are little known outside the places whose name they bear. The recipes are individual, easy, economical, readily available, and have a strong regional accent. This is Derbyshire food at its best.

£12.99

Derbyshire Walks with Children
William D Parke

There are 24 circular walks, ranging from 1 to 6 miles in length, and each one has been researched and written with children in mind. The directions and background information have been checked and revised as necessary for this updated reprint.

Detailed instructions for parents and an interactive commentary for children mean there's never a dull moment. There are even 'escape routes' to allow families to tailor each walk to suit their own needs, time and energy.

"The needs, entertainment and safety of children have been of paramount importance."
– Peak Advertiser

£8.99

All-Terrain Pushchair Walks:
The Peak District
Alison Southern

The Peak District, in the heart of the country, has some of England's most picturesque landscapes, from the White Peak in the south with its rocky outcrops and steep hills, to the Dark Peak in the north with peat moss moorland and stunning vistas. This book is for families with all-terrain pushchairs and buggies, and for everyone wishing to avoid as many stiles and obstacles as possible. Includes family-friendly attractions, trees to identify, birds and plants to spot, and lots more to discover. Have fun while you walk enjoying the amazing views, have some healthy exercise and spend time with the family away from the modern world.

£7.95.

Peak District Trigpointing Walks
Hill walking with a point to it!
Keith Stevens & Peter Whittaker

A superb introduction to an intriguing new walking experience: searching out all those elusive Ordnance Survey pillars. Packed with detailed walks to new and interesting Peak District summits, with a wealth of fascinating information on the history of the OS and the art of GPS navigation.

There are 150 Peak District Ordnance Survey pillars — can you find them all? Walk to all the best scenic viewpoints — from the top you can spot all the surrounding pillars. This book shows you how.

£8.95

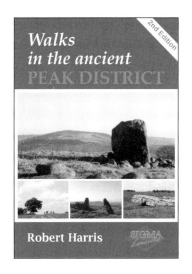

Walks in the Ancient Peak District
Robert Harris

A collection of walks visiting the prehistoric monuments and sites of the Peak District. A refreshing insight into the thinking behind the monuments, the rituals and strange behaviour of our ancestors. All the routes are circular, most starting and finishing in a town or village that is easy to locate and convenient to reach by car.

£8.99

Discovering Manchester
2nd Edition
Barry Worthington

This stylish walking guide doubles as a detailed account of the city's architecture, its history and tourism attractions. There are walks throughout Manchester including such major entertainment and cultural centres as the Bridgewater Hall, Urbis, the Museum of Science and Industry, the Lowry and many more. Explore the entire city – from the Corn Exchange to G-Mex, from the Cathedral to Affleck's Palace.
£10.99

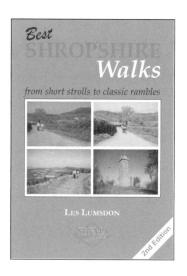

Best Shropshire Walks 2nd Edition
From short strolls to classic rambles
Les Lumsdon

A new revised edition of this much loved guide contains 36 walks, including 12 completely new routes, located in all parts of the county. Several walks feature fine hill walking on the Welsh borders and others start from delightful villages and hamlets in the north and east of the county.
£8.99

Beatrix Potter's Derwentwater
Joyce Irene Whalley and Wynne Bartlett

A fascinating look at the beautiful Derwentwater area as Beatrix Potter depicted in her sketches and books. Includes paintings and sketches by Beatrix Potter and photographs both old and new make this an invaluable book for visitors to the Lake District, and all those who know and love Peter Rabbit and his friends.

Detailed routes are included for three walks starting from Keswick so readers can explore the wonderful scenery found in the stories of Benjamin Bunny, Squirrel Nutkin and Mrs Tiggie-winkle.

£9.99

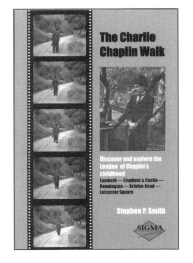

The Charlie Chaplin Walk
Stephen P Smith

Explore the London streets of Charlie Chaplin's childhood in a chronological tour that can be taken on foot or from the comfort of an armchair. This book concentrates on the story of Chaplin's formative years and takes a fresh look at the influence they had upon his films. For fans of Chaplin, those interested in film history and anybody with an interest of the social history of London's poor of the late Victorian and early Edwardian era.

£9.99

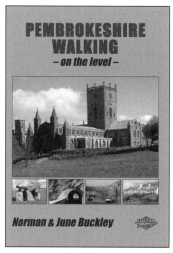